SAD DAYS OF LIGHT

Also by Peter Balakian
Father Fisheye

SAD DAYS OF LIGHT

poems by

Peter Balakian

*To Joyce,
with all the best wishes
for a happy birthday.
Sincerely,
Peter Balakian*

**The Sheep Meadow Press
New York**

ACKNOWLEDGMENTS

Grateful acknowledgment is made to the editors of the following publications in which these poems have appeared:

Ararat: "The Secret"; *Carolina Quarterly:* "Granny, Making Soup," "O Little Sister"; *Colorado Quarterly:* "Three Museum Offerings"; *Confrontation:* "The Stuffing: East Orange, New Jersey, 1942"; *The Greenfield Review:* "Road to Aleppo, 1915"; *The Literary Review:* "First Nervous Breakdown, Newark 1941," "What My Grandmother Said When It Rained"; *Poetry Northwest:* "The History of Armenia," "For My Grandmother Coming Back," "Ocean Markings/The New Year"; *Rhode Island Review:* "Remembering Grandmother's Music," "Diarbekir, Turkey, 1914: How It Was Then"

"The Field of Poppies" first appeared in *New Directions in Prose and Poetry 38* (New Directions Publishing Corp., 1979)

Library of Congress Cataloging in Publication Data

Balakian, Peter, 1951-
    Sad days of light.

    1. Armenian Americans — Poetry.   I. Title.
PS3552.A443S2 1983   811'.54   82-10823
ISBN 0-935296-33-6
ISBN 0-935296-34-4 (pbk.)

To the memory of my grandmother
*   Nafina Aroosian*
Diarbekir, Armenia, 1890 - Englewood, New Jersey, 1964;
In memoriam, my grandfather
*   Diran Balakian*
Tokad, Armenia, 1877 - New York City, 1939

And the spirits of all the dead, tonight,
Through my own eyes and soul,
Are awaiting the dawning of the light,
So that, to humanize the cruelty
Of our inhuman lives,
Perhaps from above a drop of light
May fall upon the murdered and the murderer alike.

Siamanto

Contents

I

II

III

✳

I

The History of Armenia

Last night
my grandmother returned
in her brown dress
standing on Oraton Parkway
where we used to walk
and watch the highway
being dug out.
She stood against
a backdrop of steam hammers
and bulldozers,
a bag of fruit
in her hand,
the wind blowing
through her eyes.

I was running
toward her
in a drizzle
with the morning paper.
When I told her
I was hungry, she said,
in the grocery store
a man is standing
to his ankles in blood,
the babies in East Orange
have disappeared
maybe eaten by
the machinery
on this long road.

When I asked for my mother
she said gone,
all gone.

3

The girls went for soda,
maybe the Coke was bad,
the candy sour.
This morning the beds
are empty, water off,
the toilets dry.
When I went to the garden
for squash
only stump was there,
when I went to clip
parsley
only a hole.

We walked past piles
of gray cinder and cement
trucks, there were no men.
She said Grandpa left
in the morning
in the dark;
he had pants to press
for the firemen of
East Orange.
They called him
in the middle of night,
West Orange was burning
Montclair was burning
Bloomfield and Newark
were gone.

One woman carried
the arms of her child
to East Orange last night
and fell on her uncle's
stoop, two boys came
with the skin
of their legs

in their pockets
and turned themselves in
to local officials;
this morning sun
is red and spreading.

If I go to sleep
tonight, she said,
the ceiling will open
and bodies will fall
from clouds. *Yavrey*
where is the angel,
where is the angel
without sword, *yavrey*
where is the angel
without six fingers
and a missing leg
where is the angel
with the news that the river
is coming back,
the angel with the word
that the water will be clear
and have fish.

Grandpa is pressing
pants, they came for him
before the birds were up—
he left without shoes
or tie, without shirt
or suspenders.
It was quiet
the birds, the birds
were still sleeping.

Seferis Returning to Smyrna

As you approach,
the thread of shore
is whiter
than the sky.
Fishing boats cast no shadows
and the lighthouse stands
as a cylinder of salt.

The street you take
from harbor is shrunken.
Your legs are numb
as if the merchant selling fruit
recognized your eyes.

Past the courtyard
of St. Nicholas
now remade into a school,
almond trees are stump.
The pomegranates you smelled
as flaming juice
when you sneaked
along the wharf to catch
the night-barge to Marseilles—
are now light stains
beneath your feet.

In your grandmother's garden
where the widows sat
to watch the light fall
on the silent harbor,
the trellis draped

with grapes returns a scent
of your brother's hair and shirt.

The fig trees,
where the votive rags
were tied, still hang
with the stink
of smoking fruit
that rose like a hole
in the high blue sky—

and still lingers in the creases
of your clothes.

All evening you walk the streets,
loukoumades rising hot and sweet
in your nose,
the hollow villas falling
in your arms—
a man like your uncle
rummaging a roofless house,

and the harbor
full of skin and wind
sends back a breath
and the lighthouse
loses shape
against the sky.

Road to Aleppo, 1915

There must have
been a flame
like a leaf
eaten in the sun,
that followed you—
a white light
that rose higher
than the mountain
and singed the corner
of your eye
when you turned
to find the screaming
trees dissolving
to the plain.

Even when the sun
dropped, there was a heat
like the ground
of needles stirring
up your legs,
and in a light
and dying wind
the throats of boys
droning like the sheep
beyond the hill
kept ringing
in your ears.

The silence
of the ground
filled the high
empty sky.
Your breath
like horizon
settled into black,
and you stuttered
every mile
to your daughter's
shorter step—

the moaning air
almost gone
filled inside
your dress.

Granny, Making Soup

In its stone pores
this pot holds
what is left of time—
the herbs

early mint, dill, walnut-root,
the dust of the rusty stick of cinnamon
that we pass from generation
to generation;

run your finger along
the curve, it is soft
like a fine shell,
smell the bottom,
it is stronger
than when my grandmother
rubbed it with her palm.

*

I break the shoulder bones
apart, no knife, nothing metal—
the white ball of the joint
we'll all chew later.
Now, the socket
from which it is pulled
is the empty round
where we join.

I hacked three times a week
a lamb like this
for market—
the oldest daughter
did this for her father

and I knew when
their blue throats
swallowed in my hand,
how close we were to soup,

and when the pink-gray skin,
shaved and glowing
in the sun
was slit and wheezing
and crying out its guts,
I watched papa
take a fingerful of blood
and bring it to his nose.

*

Here, the white string
the teeth
cannot cut
must be left,

you must take the tendon
and give it to the water
of the soup.

When I see it
in the cauldron
like a frazzled strand of fish,
I think how like
the body fiber
is the ankle of a goat
who wanders
on the dry steppe
for weeks and weeks
until from some small cave
there is water
thin and clear singing
along the sand

11

and we drink,
we all drink.

*

When the water rises
in this pot
and a slow steam
comes over the clean bones
and shoulder fat,
there is a low gurgle
and the marrow moves.
The flecks of basil open
like small leaves
and the celery grows dark,
softens and bends
its head
like a weed
for bottom.

I have watched this, Peter,
through the dark stone
of cauldron,
and when there was no light,
a first steam started—
I could hear the grain
in my spoon settle
and my hair tightened
as in August
on the wharf.

In an hour my daughters
will sneak in to smell,
grandpa will loosen
his shirt,
the plants will droop

but now,
all is at bottom
and coming.

*

Always in afternoon
you let the pot alone

the water will take
from the bones
what the lamb takes from the earth.

The water will take
from the marrow
what the lamb's small mouth
takes from the low hills:
the high grass
beyond the wet meadow
and the weeds around
the eucalyptus.
And in night
when the lamb takes
the young fig
and breaks its sac
so the seed will
cover ground—

this too
the water takes
from the bones.

And when the lamb
wanders beyond the steppe
to the first ledge
of the mountain,

and the wildcat pins
him to the dust
and dry red shale,
and tears him
almost woolless
until the baby's bleat
of his throat is hushed,
and his organs are gnashed
to nothing,
and he is open
and clean of everything
but the long bones
of his back
thinner than the cat's teeth,
and the blood
dries on the skin
and the feathers
of gray wool are left
for the birds to smell—

this too
the water takes
from the bones

*

And when we return
in evening,
the water will be full
of the stone
and like a voice
it will moan
with its tendon, fat, and bone,
and with the little meat
we've left for our own teeth,

and then, Peter,
we'll have broth —

and when you
take it to your lips,
you will take it
all in.

Diarbekir, Turkey, 1914:
How It Was Then

in the far province
on the lake
with a man who entered
your house each night,
a day of dark
green water
in his hair.

The silence of your legs
in bed,
and the low breathing
of slow sheep
on the slopes
where the sun would
leave and drop
through your window.

Your only child
dumb to everything
but the bees
in the fattest flowers,

to her there was
no difference
between high grass
and the lace
you made for her arms

how could it matter;
you watched
the black night
rise over your head
and felt the stars
moving in your
husband's sea.

16

First Nervous Breakdown, Newark 1941

In the street, she said,
you were walking
past a laundry
muttering to the shirts
hanging without heads
in the window

and when you walked
into the store
you kicked the empty
pants and asked for legs.

Outside the butcher's
those were cows' eyes
and moon-fat black balls
you took and gathered
to your chest
as if to say without
a word, they were alive
and beckoning for care.

And the hanging ribs
fresh and red
with the bright white
bone like a scythe
running through—
she said you hit it
with your cane
until it screamed.

Then you disappeared
in a crowd off
the bus and gave away
tomatoes and pears,
and walked with
the last stranger
to a far apartment
by the bridge
and sat looking down
by the water.

Remembering Grandmother's Music

Once far from your small
daughter's sleep,
the cake in your throat —
coffee green
as the walls
that showed your eyes,

the tables of faces
droned like the bad
music of Newark.

How the angel
making music with the dishes
in the back room
passed the sweet juice
of the lamb to the old men
outside by the neon, *Eat,*

the men who played
all night with their last teeth
the song of four boys
you left by the lake
with a dead man
cradled in their arms —

a choir of hairless throats
you heard each night
the dock's tide rocked
your shivering breasts
to sleep in Marseilles

where your daughter called
papa to each dark sailor
and with her squeeze
asked for the
sweet fruit.

The Stuffing: East Orange, New Jersey, 1942

When she returned
with the red-net sack,
slumped on the porch
and looked to the buildings
falling in thick air, she
told her daughter:

high country,
village at its feet,

tonight we take
the goat's stomach
and fist it full
of lamb, onion
and the secret guts —
take fine high grass
from the steppe
and powder it to dust.

Use your palm,
small one,
to crush the garlic's
purple knob,
press the white heart
into the cup
of your hand.

When you slit
the black lip of olive,
take the pit,
and when the night
falls on your window
place it in your cheek
and suck.

When we press the juice
from the walnut
and mince the husk
a light dust
will rise from
our ankles

and you, dear heart,
will feel a clear oil
run the tips
of your fingers
and know your father's
scent—
the light perfume
in your palm.

In the Turkish Ward

*(in memoriam: my grandfather
Diran Balakian, 1877-1939)*

*for my father and my aunts
Anna and Nona*

1

Over my head the fan moves slowly.
Ceiling lights flicker and dizz.
The corridor door opens and closes,
stirs the medicinal vapors which hang
all night over these damp bodies;
the air settles on everything. All week
I've wrapped heads, arms, numb legs,
the ointment on my hands is red.
I smell the Turkish boots in the hall,
piles of brown canvas pants.

2

They give me nothing—not bread, tea.
The guards leer at me when I come and go.
"When they're asleep and you're waiting
for the day, you'll want some sweet—
small plums and figs." I should listen
to my wife. They stare at me,
these wounded, swelling in their sleep.
An Armenian doctor conscripted in
the Turkish army, "our only way to stay
alive," my wife reminds me in my sleep.

23

3

For three days the sirocco slows
over the channel, the iridescent dirty water.
Boats unload. All day I wandered market
to square, the smell of carbolic trailing me.
Fruit gone to sear: strawberries dead-ripe,
slit currants, the sodden heads of melons
I could bandage with my hands. The cores,
rind, pits along the wharf...a man's eyes,
a dead man's eyes. If I could find some
fine dyed silk for my daughter...

4

East and West, the great circle propped
on two half-hemispheres, Sophia.
Hagia Sophia. The water might well leak
into what used to be the apse and rise
along the whitewashed tiles—disclose
the robes translucent, mute eyes,
glittering acanthus. O unhealthy tide,
grout the cherubim lost in the dome.
This sea should rise into the basilica
of light pouring each day from the open eye
upon the backs of the groaning in prayer.

5

Yesterday, bloody news from my friend,
the poet, Siamanto. I must know what I believe.
"The Ottoman sticks deeper in the heartland:
all night; screaming infants lit like candles,
the wheat full of body parts and clothes.
The riverside is Armenia wafted by a soundless
desert air. This firmament is blind...
shrieking in the dawn, Mother, one fell swoop,
the herds become debris, hills a heap of flesh

what leaks from the midnight air of Anatolia,
my good friend, I'm too weak to say."

6

I'm hemmed here. The Allies like sump
in the harbor. If I could shake one British
Admiral, he'd not believe this tale—
a hundred miles from his bow. Here, a poet's
words, "Armenia is a scarlet herb, a walking
shadow." Each letter he says, "look upon your
surgeon's skill and your conscription
as a blessing, we need you in the city
to help us with night passage out."

7

Another day of waste. Even at this dull night-
hour I smell the sun inland. These cots,
pillows, sheets of phlegm, sallow heads.
"Father, what are you, your hands; each night
in the Sultan's den...men whose teeth
fall apart with our flesh. Tonight
who knows, have I a cousin left?" Each night
dear daughter, I write this letter in my head

in the brown dawn, the poet's voice—a cat's
out on the steppe...I need a cistern
for my yellow bile. "Stay close to the docks...
three men, a family, to Athens, Marseilles."

Sweet one, what's fate—to hold arms
by healing, force my blood to pitch
because to face each night here
is not to know whose blood is whose.

8

There are sacred secrets, Hippocrates,
you could not dream of. What is Law in
my Art; my speculum, stethoscope, the mirror
banded to my head; if these instruments
vanished, would I let the dying go?
Would my hands dissolve?

Good Moor, Christian Moor, unhappy Moor,
what course led you to this chidden sea.
What dog set your heart upon itself;
in this room your wife's tears are mere water.

If my daughter knew how my hands tremor,
how a scant tendon keeps my heart from
dropping through my bottom . . . in this hour

the heavy air settles on the wharf and windows,
close to my head, I hear the whole town . . .
nothing — plashing water, wind in the moorings.

What My Grandmother Said When It Rained

We knew they were coming.
All night we could hear machetes
whirring in our ears.
The Turks gave themselves away;
they drank all night,
and in the morning beat the horses.

So Papa took all the money and jewels:
the fat gold coins, the turquoise,
braids of gold chains we'd wear once
a year, rings silver and almost soft,
and the brooches from Greece, topaz,
onyx, jade.
There were stones of colors
you cannot name,
I can still see them . . .

He packed them all
into the ceiling,
into the dark space above the house.
I always thought the devil
lived there.
Papa hid them all
in the ceiling,
and told us someday,
someday we'll return
and be rich again.

Sometimes when it rains,
when the sun shakes behind the clouds
and the summer air cools
so the windows darken,
I hear God with a fist full
of coins in his big wild hand—

I hear them spill in a mountain
over the floor of dark air
above the clouds—
the shaking gold pieces,
the gems deep green
like my husband's eye.

For My Grandmother, Coming Back

For the dusty rugs
and the dye of blue-roots,
for the pale red stomachs of sheep,
you come back.

For the brass ladle
and the porous pot of black
from your dinner of fires,
I call your name like a bird.

For the purple fruit
for the carrots like cut fingers
for the riverbed damp
with flesh,
you come back.

For the field of goats
wet and gray,
for the hoofs and sharp bones
floating in the broth,
I wave my arms full of wind.

For the tumbling barrel
of red-peppers,
for the milled mountain of wheat
for the broken necks
of squash fat and full of seed,
I let my throat open.

For the lips of young boys
bitten through
for the eyes of virgins brown
and bleating on the hill,
for the petticoat of your daughter
shivering by the lake,
for the yarn of her arms
unwinding at her father's last shout.

For the lamb punctured
from the raw opening
to his red teeth,
for the lamb rotating
like the sun
on its spit,
for the eyes that fall
into the fire,
for the tongue tender and full,
for the lungs smoldering
like leaves
and the breasts spilling
like yellow milk
and the stomach heaving
its fist full of days
like red water falling
into the stream,

I wave my arms full of birds
full of dry gusts
full of burning clothes,
and you come back,
you come back.

II

The Claim

Application for the support of
Claims AGAINST FOREIGN GOVERNMENTS

May 15, 1919 Department of State

The light, perfumed wind
off the Park,
oaks and chestnuts
arched over Fifth Avenue.
Today I am the age
she was in 1915

history is a man's breath,
whatever I take in I give out
the mother of my mother

her wobbly skeletal frame
  all about me
the high-pitched calcium
  of the bones
in the atmosphere I breathe

> Q.1. Give the (a) name, (b) residence, and (c) occupation
> A.1. (a) Nafina Hagop Chilinguirian (born Sheker-
>   lemedjian) (b) Ghuri st. Aleppo, Syria. (c) Tailoress.
>
> Q.2. nature and extent of life, interest, lien, mortgage
>   inclusive dates . . . right, title, interest
>
> A.2. (a) complete ownership (b) Since August 1915
>   (c) From my husband Hagop Chilinguirian, the
>   original claimant who was a citizen of U.S.A.
>   beginning his minority till the year 1901 A.D. when

he returned in order to arrange his affairs but he
died during our deportation
written in detail in
the answers

my head feathery
in the hot June wind.

My grandmother used to say:
they went there—
they were going
to the river Tigris.

—relatives
who are perished on account of the deportation
leaving me and my brother Thomas Shekerlemedjian
now residing at
U.S.A.
Box 125 West Hoboken New Jersey

(Answer Question 15 c)

I, Lucia Der Hovsepian, 45 years old, born in Diarbekir
Turkey, residing in Zeki st. Aleppo, Syria, occupying
by domestic works residing before the deportation
in Diarbekir, do solemnly affiirm that Nafina Hagop
Chilinguirian had her birth certificate

all over Central Park today   hydrangea opening

but it was lost during the deportation; that she is
born in Diarbekir, Turkey, at 22nd Oct. 1890 of the
parents Hagop Shekerlemedjian and Lucia Nadjarian.

who deprived me of my ripe years? who?
I heard her say this once behind
closed doors,

but when I walked into
the room no one else was there
walls, no moldings   rugs around her
Bokhara   magenta   Kashan   flowers on sand

(A) GENERAL QUESTIONS
14. state race to which claimant belongs
    Armenian, white

    22 October 1890 Diarbekir   Turkey
    my birth certificate was lost
    attached the affidavit for

17. give causes or purposes

A.17. My husband and I were about to depart for
    U.S.A. but the roads were closed
    on account of the war, so I was obliged to
    rest in Aleppo, Syria after the deportation

    my husband Hagop Chilinguirian
    being dead on the way

She must have filed
the claim twice and failed,
my aunt said, and
for sixty years—
in the third drawer
of the dresser...

            a peak where Noah landed
            dove come back
            with a twig

            Ararat with a twig

spice mountain
spice mountain

to see the nose become
powder and the hair dust

    that my husband was a citizen...
        but as for the record concerning the date and place
of his Naturalization please be kind to ask of
the gentleman whose name and address I am giving
below... Mr. S. Solokdjian

    We the undersigned of this affidavit
do solemnly affirm that Hagop Chilinguirian
       the husband of Nafina
is of the U.S.A. for when he was living frequently
we heard of himself... having his Naturalization
and Passport which he did show us

Here, on this steamy
island, I smell the mood
of another place:
the oil rags of women
ferried from home

red unguent   crow-beak   anise   eucalyptus

       leave by the stable
       the lake is fire

    I pere Harutiun Yessayan, the Prelate of Armenians
in Aleppo... do hereby certify that I have no
interest in the claim
                PRELATURE   ALEP   1919

I used to roll grapeleaves
with her   Sunday after Church;

we washed off the brine
cut the thick stem out.

SECTION V
FACTS REGARDING CLAIM

Q.55. Give an itemized statement ... description
of property entirely lost   description of
damage   value in dollars American   losses

2500 kg. of sugar a 3 p. gold	750 Ltq.
household furniture	250
goods left at my husband's shop	
1000 kg. of sugar	500
5000 kg. of coffee a 15 p. gold	750
2000 kg. of hemp-cords	100
1000 parcels of sacks	250
1000 curry-combs a 5 p. gold	750
25000 kegs of rice	750
6000 kegs gall-nut	100

Ready money robbed on the way by the Turks
The money necessary to rear my two daughters,
Gladys 7 years old and Alice 5 years old
   till their marriage   2000

The carrion of a soup
coppery urine on my fingers;

       horse screams   go back
       curry-combs   mane   meat stink

My grandmother's voice
reverberations off the walls
walls where nations disappear
the walls around Diarbekir
walls around   around
walls   a trellis of grapes

TOTAL IN GOLD   5900 Ltq.

  my husband Hagop   of sufferings on the way   350

    Changed into American dollars at the rate of
    that time in 1915 A.D.   68750 dollars

The hedges in the Park filling me
like an aphrodisiac;
the ripe years
the swelling
fruit in her

bowls of pears   mangoes
avocados   lumpy peaches
a body

    list of the losses and injuries come down

     by inheritance from our relatives
       indicated below

My brother Harutuin Shekerlemedjian, merchant
...had at Karadja Hagh a village in Diarbekir
150 tons of rice kept in three wells   captured
by the government   3500 Ltq.   in his shop at the
market-place goods: calicoes, cloths, silken clothes
the shop at Iz-ed-din:
    cotton-clothes,
    calicoes, leathers
500 sheep   village Talavli

jewels and money possessed by my relatives
mentioned below...kept under the ground in a
 box

The blood value for a person
    was ordered to be 350 Ltq.
    by decree of the Sultan

I feel the jackal
in my pants.

    at my sister's house Hadji Anna...
    captured by Turk named Hadji Bakkar

        take nothing house
        burning   horse   flame

(C) My father Hagop Shekerlemedjian, 75 years old,
    killed by Turks

My mother Lucia Shekerlemedjian, 50 years old,
                killed by Turks   350
My brother Dikran Shekerlemedjian, 35 years old,
                killed by Turks   350
His son Karnig Shekerlemedjian, 7 years old,
                killed by Turks   350

My tongue is dark with coffee

        eat, this is good for you,
        only oil of olive
        nothing meat

His son Diran Shekerlemedjian, 4 years old,
                killed by Turks   350
My brother Harutiun Shekerlemedjian, 30 years old,
                killed by Turks   350
His son Levon Sherkerlemedjian, 2 years old,
                killed by Turks   350
His daughter Azniv Sherkerlemedjian, 5 years old,
                killed by Turks   350

My sister Hadji Anna Derhovsepian, 28 years old,
　　　　　killed by Turks　　　　　　350
My sister Arusyag Berberian, 25 years old,
　　　　　killed by Turks　　　　　　350

By the lofty cedars of Lebanon
and the oaks of Bashan
there I used to lie
when I was a girl

We the undersigned of this affidavit, Thomas Alchikian 50
years old, Armenian shoemaker and Yervant Ekmekdjian
35, Armenian blacksmith solemnly affirm
　　　　　that Nafina Hagop Chilinguirian
is the very owner...

Pick them from the vine with
care, she would say—
the tender ones,
light green.

Now I see the vines,
a web: lamb-tongue　cow-foot　human eye

The tulips are blinding
whole rows, streaks
along 64th street
like a smear
of poppies

　　　　　my husband in spite of that he was
　　a citizen of U.S.A. was forced...as he was
　　feable and indisposed being subjected to

such conditions
and seeing our relatives

killed inhumanly, he could not
    support the life and died

    leaving me a widow with my two orphan daughters
        Gladys 7 years old and Alice 5

    We the remaining deportees, women and children
    were forced to walk without being allowed even
    to buy some bread to eat. Frequently we were
    robbed by Turks as if they would carry us safely
    to our destiny which was entirely unknown

    So for thirty days we were obliged to wander
    through mountains and valleys   fatigue and hunger
    enforced by the whip of the gendarmes diminshed
    the number of deportees

        my brothers' heads are
        on the vine, on the vine;
        what rots is in the pot

    after many dangers whose description would take
    much time a few women and children included I my-
    self arrived at Aleppo Syria beginning September 1915

    that the Turk people plundered and captured
        that they are all killed by the Turks during
    our deportation . . . except

Sunday in the summer
  The Father and the Son,
he said, granny, and the ghost too
you told me

    Mrs. Nafina's husband who died of violent
    sufferings caused by the unhuman cruelties
    of the deporter gendarmes

QUESTION 63

facts of circumstance
  attending losses or injuries

1 August 1915 our parish in Diarbekir was besieged
by the gendarmes...the same day with the menace of
death they removed us, the Armenians

We could take by us only our ready money, if it was
easy to take, our birth and marriage certificates;
my husband's Naturalization Paper and Passport

I never knew why you
were in Marseilles in 1919

> *the harbor, women waiting,*
> *docks with light*

by their allowance the Turk people plundered and
captured our goods   the deporter gendarmes separated
the men from the women and binding them to each
other, they carried all of us to an unknown direction.

The trellis of grapevines
in the apartment courtyard;
now I see them for what
they are

> After three days of journey, they killed one by one
> the man deportees of whom only a few were saved.
> So were killed mercilessly my brothers and sisters and

Sunday her coat like incense
in Armenian we do not say

for ever and ever. Amen.
it means unto the Ages of Ages.

Since then I am supported by the Hon. Consulate
of U.S.A. at Aleppo

I remember when
she helped me blow
the candles out,
my fifth birthday;
no light, only curls
of smoke in
the dark kitchen.

The deportation and the fiendish steps taken
against the Armenians in general being well
known by the civilized world, I do not mention
other evidences concerning this matter
    Only
        I assert that:

how long will they cook   the eyes   the eyes of men
where is the Black sea   is the sea Black
why do women wear black to Church

I am a human being ... it was impossible to
have by me the documentary evidence concerning my
losses but my co-deportees saved from death
witness that
        I am
I am human   herewith affidavit.

III

My Aunt Gladys Who Carries the Kitchen

It is always at night,
I see you in the empty yard
with a broom—
the wind billowing your dress

the voice of your mother
in the chill
whispering, *sleep*

and the tree which is
your mother's dress
blooming from the dry flowers
of the village square.

*

I hear you alone rise
in the night
with the clatter of wares:

the brass ladle,
iron pots, the deep black
dishes of your father;
the knives with bone-handles,
forks missing a tooth,
the bowls, the wooden bowls
thumbed and rubbed
to a dust bottom.

Around you, always around you
the barrels full and dark
with sour vines and tomato cuts,
the leaves of the grape thin as skin.

You rise with the small cups,
the fine handles of the small cups
chipped and missing,
the white china
that is the bottom of the small cups
on which the mud of the coffee dries:
the silt from which your mother
read the water's mark —

the saucers with filigree
yellow like the flower of your sister's hair.

You rise with the green copper
of the mortar and pestle
still working like a joint —
the clove, the mustard seed, the pepper
like a black eye, the full wheat
ground and worked to powder.

I hear you aunt Gladys,
the carrier of this kitchen
the carrier of the invisible wall of fat,
of the steam ceiling rising
from your back —
the floor of scraps and peelings,
dying turnips, eggplant gone to seed
rising over your ankles.

I hear you my aunt
at the tub, the sink that is a tub
where the water fills

where the cold potatoes float and open,
where the radish and the headless celery swell
and the liver and the veins
and the tissue of the stomach
soak for the night —
for the dinner of silence.

And the hands,
the hands of dust,
the hands of vinegar and oil
the hands of the wet mouths
of the dogs of Van,
the hands of your mother
full of lips and saliva
full of urine and dirt
full of the silent eyes of the cows
and the boys who will no more speak.

*

This is the sink
you come to, my aunt, in the night
when you scrub the roots and tubers
of the earth,
when you take the cold water
of the deep night to your wrists
and let the arms sink
into the rinsings of the food—

into the beet-deep cold
we eat and gnaw
and chatter on.

Can I Tell My Limping Aunt

Can I tell my limping aunt
her dress is for eternity,
or for some butterfly weed
along the edge of the road?

She is in the kitchen
every day before the dullest
morning casts a light
on the geraniums and hydrangea
in her yard.

Though I am a hundred miles away,
I know it is still dark
when she wakes and turns
the kitchen faucet on
to break the silence.

I think of her this morning
as I rise;
the cold rain in my breath.
The darkness in the hall
stops me in my own warm steps.

I think of the deep rust mums
and the creeping cyclamen around
her garden walk,
and what sweet lovers they've
been all October.

I know the petunias
bright blue and purple-faced
as her apron
kept her over the sink

for hours
polishing tumblers
over and over until
the sun went down.

When I think of her
this morning in the kitchen
dragging her leg from sink
to table to cutting board,
through the hall of empty bottles,
hovering over the cupboards
dusting the cans

I want to say:
the mortal flowers
on your dress,
the pansies and dandelions
the daisy and the tulip

they are not a child's drifting world
or a young girl's bouquet
in disorder from the wind;
they are not the petals
on the bridal floor
where you stood and watched
your sisters handed away.

Pull the dress around you
to keep the coming air
from getting in

let the petals and stems,
the silky filament and the tongues
of invisible pollen—

fall inside your dress,
fall inside your skin.

To Arshile Gorky

Cousin, uncle, brother, fellow
townsman, I come to you this day,
deported with berry soil on my hands.
Somewhere between your lake in Armenia
and this place there is a trail
of ash—almost chalk—to bring
the limbs back to fullness. Now,
your mother's stomach is dried fruit

on your palette. Though swallows
glide and turn through the rope
still hanging in your barn, in
this ghostly light you are a shadow:
off white, then gray, then a wisp
of flame rising in the dust.

The Secret

for my brother Jim

It is a secret
my brother knows;
something he cannot tell.
It is an Armenian secret.
It must be older
than the first souls
who wandered in a land
I have not seen.

It is only in the darkness
of our room
when he returns
late at night
that I see him
with his long arms
leaning against the sill,
looking out upon
the night settling.

In a shaft of moon
I see his deep eyes
somber like
Arshile Gorky's eyes.
I see what they must see
and cannot say.

*

There are shapes of people
we love in the dark —
there is night in all
the houses you can see.

Rain is drying on everything.
The beams of our room
creak and enlarge
with darkness.

You, brother, are like Gorky
drinking in this
wet night,
listening to it dry—

seeing the shape
of our father
moving in the garden,
the plot you planted
last May.

He is moving among
the bell peppers
and parsley;
he is bending
toward the soil.

You are looking out
upon windows and fences
and plots of ground
which people
claim they own.

He is walking out
into the orchard
and the drying leaves;

you smell the fruit
and some dark bud
which calls us out.

*

Out there,
our father is a shape,
and here
in the silent rooms
we must make a way.

There is a stairway
and a rug,
a familiar vase —
shapes of furniture
which echo

there are walls
which we must hold up
with our breath —
walls where brothers join.

In the morning
you will not tell me this,
you will say nothing.

The Field of Poppies

for my mother

Cypress spiral to the sky.
Painters came here because
the dirt was dry as their bones,
because even the monastery on the hill
flaked each day.
You want a picture of yourself
in this poppy field;
wind blowing the long grass
around your legs,
fields of yellow flower across
the road moving away from you.
The high mountain is where
the town's saint disappeared
with his wound.
When he returned
peach trees sprouted from rock,
and the gray clouds left the mountain.

Cypress spiral to the sky.
Your father found this field
and the mountain uncovered,
the monastery a pure glint of sun.
You want this picture
to show your body disappearing
in the red waves of flower,
a field of pin-pricks
rising and falling in the breeze,
each step spreading the red
over your joints.

You want the red to cover
the mountain,
you want the line where
sky and land meet
to turn the color of the heart.
This is how your father left;
foot, knee, stomach, face
disappearing in the stain of this field,
in the light wind that sang
in the red flowers.

O Little Sister

for my sister Janet

There is a light falling slowly
over the bushes,
and the filigree of trees
at the window is almost gone.
The small birch is thinning
to a pin,
and though I remember the bark
white, ash-white this morning,
now it is graying
like the coy squirrel's eye.

And my sister, my little sister
is pulling off the branches
for the fire—

She is gathering twigs and dry leaves,
she is taking to her chest
severed pieces of roots
and soft rotting wood the ants left.

She is taking with her hands
the rose-brier thin and purple
like the veins of her arms,
and with her wrists
I see her in the waning amber
pulling the grape-vine
and the cucumber's long rope.

O little sister,
I see you as a shape,
a soft bending tree

in the coming night air —
soon the sky will disappear

and you will know the steps
before you
as a deer finds
a distance between trees,
and you will see this window —
how empty is the pane

and learn the way the owl knows
there is a spreading light
like the fire's low flame
going cold over the kindling trees
that slip into the darkness
of their shape,
the rings of their bark.

Under The Half Moon

for my sister Pamela

I

Under the shell,
under the hen's old egg
half-bloomed
rough and white
hanging over us,
lighting the porch

night, the other half
in cleavage.

I smell the first signs
of the year's fall—
the red-choked sumac
blowing apart

the suckle's sweet
whiffed by the wind
once more
after rain.

II

You can't read
in a book
how to know,
you said this once, grandmother

a night
when rain had stopped

and we walked
the back meadow,
you said:

Harry, your uncle Harry
would take his pile
of green beans
and shiny white onions

and on this stump
this same
soft ash
he'd chop and slice,

and tell me
how a night like this,
one you smell
like this—
when the ground
letting go its wet
would rise
into your hair
so you could smell
what was dying

the aster, phlox,
the hollyhock

and he would say to me,
little sister,
think how on a night
like this
in the old world
papa would stack
the squat logs,
chop the dry hemlock,

twist and bend
the eucalyptus
like a rope,
then carry
in his arms like a baby
the brush:

vines with shriveled
grapes,
the stale olive twigs,
blackened fig leaves
and those dead-neck flowers
mama would keep forever.

And when he
brought the lantern
to ignite
the first straw
we shivered
with the whole night.

And when the flame caught
and spread
like a traveling vine,
like a blowing tree
in the noon sun,

his big hands
would rise
and for a moment
we'd lose him
in the fire.

*

When it all calmed
and burned even

we'd quiet and start
to sing,
all of us
like shaking plants
in the wind...

mama would bring
the pots full of gizzards
and boiled roots,
and the wooden bowl
full of rice.

In the morning we'd
collect the ash—
it had a fine scent,
little sister,

mama would gather it
to season the iron pots
and mix with the incense
for Sunday—

she'd even throw
a pinch
for the chickens.

*

And yesterday, grandson,
when I cut
the chickens,
when I took the knife
to their throats

and the blood spilled
to the ground
till the birds
were empty
and twitching,

I thought of how
all blood is the same—
how when you've cradled
one neck,
when blood
has spilled
through your hands
once,
it will spill
again and again
until the fingers
are like gnarled roots
knotted inside themselves
twitching
and almost limp
as wet feathers.

*

Harry would chop
his beans all night,
slice and chop
for the stew—
on this old ash stump.

And he'd sing
and how the wind
filled his face,

how Harry could sing
and he always
sang to me
on a night
like this.

Three Museum Offerings

for my aunts Gladys and Alice

1

This crucifixion made from cottonwood
gnarls at the base.
The pain is in the grain of wood.
The feet twist where the root was pulled
from the ground.
A crown of thorns from brier, ruddled
and twined around the head.

In certain towns in the Southwest
a woman dressed as death
danced for three days
before falling to her feet
at the foot of this cross.

*

Accept the rib I remove from his chest.
They stirred red ochre with it
to paint the woman's bones
and then returned it to its place
on the cross.

2

This wooden mask
kept winter out of the Eskimos' blood.
The hue of green around the eyes
kept the face from disappearing into snow.

When a woman came to the shaman
with her sick child,
he stalked the tundra for twenty days
and wandered out over hard water.
When he returned with ovaries of fish,
seals reappeared and the Kuskowin broke open.

*

Accept this shell that covered
his cheekbone, and this piece of mouth
blushed and open.

3

This spear weathered and white was used
by Indians of the Plains to drain and cut.
It bled bad dreams, delirium, and ghosts.

When a mother came from her sleep in fever,
two infants strapped to her legs,
the skin of her parents in ash;
the medicine man slit her arm
and drank blood.

*

Accept this bone handle worn and smooth
and this chip of slate that is red.
It still cuts skin.

Ocean Markings/The New Year

for aunt Lucille

Everything's frozen to bottom;
scallop shells ridged in place
the spine of each sanddollar split,
small August drift like iron
on the jetty.
Each wave that breaks on shore
returns nothing.

You come back to this,
to the level of ocean
and find gulls white as ice
scanning the low tide.
You hear the wind slam
the doors of empty bathhouses.
The hedge that bloomed tiger-lily
now winds like capillary around the rail.
Even the grease from May's Drive-In is dead.

Tonight you'll let the shadow
of your mother hobbling along the wall
return to sand.
You'll come and lay the bones of your father
in the last imprint of the crab,
and return the eyes of your sister
to the pearl white shells
that know the deep weed beyond the jetty.

If you stare into the loud black waves
that claim and reclaim the moonlit rows of shells
emptied of their meat,
you'll hear the sound of birds

too far off to be familiar.
Think of their wings poised in the wind
making a long silent arc
against the furious air.

The New World: Spring Lake, New Jersey, 1925

The morning tide is red
and spills its weed
and algae on the unwalked sand.

I walked here so many
mornings of my youth;
now they seem
as one long day.

Spring Lake, I say out loud
to you, granny,
boardwalk, sand,
picket fences—
a promise for the wandering.

Like a white opal
in the sun, this beach
where your three daughters
(my mother yet to come)

could walk all day
and return to find you
sleeping under a green
striped umbrella.

The hemp-cords and rice,
curry-combs and gall nuts
gone; the brooches and jade
buried in the clay of Armenia—

your family a cup
of ash blown into the desert.

Under your umbrella,
you sleep past that place:
a dark vine on God's tree.

*

When I close my eyes
I see you slowly slipping
out of your heavy clothes.

The first Coke signs
and hot dog stands,
small bungalows uncharred
and without a human skull
on the steps—
in the backdrop.

You are undoing the back
buttons of your dress,
unlacing your shoes,

you are rolling down
the stockings that walked
alone toward Syria in 1915.

I see you taking off
your slip, the silk
mouldering with the dead
who are scattered like ewes
and rams in the outer dark
of a gray region on the map.

When I open my eyes
in this clear July light
you are taking off
your undergarments—

the handmade cotton
of another world,

you are taking off the lace
still clinging to your skin,
the lace of southeast Armenia—
a walled city,
a name too hard to hear:

let me say it for you,
Diarbekir, and for the sake
of the map, the twentieth
century map, let me say it once—
Turkey.

*

I see you in the midsummer
heat walking toward
the plunging manes
of the shoreline—
undoing your hair,
casting away the pins
and clips of a lost world,

wresting off the opal ring
of Byzantium so its white
will be etched away
by the sand.

I see your first steps
into the foam,

the periwinkles and starfish
tossed at your feet,
the weed stranded
at your ankles—

scallop shells
ridged and opalescent
filling with light.

You enter the new world
uncertain of all
save that you enter.

The lamentation of the sea
with its undercurrent
whining beneath the surf.

The waves thundering
down on you
like a covenant.

A step forward and this cobalt
sea will pass into you;
the rock breaking water
the stinging foam

a deep lucid blue
with a garland of mackerel
gulls rising and setting
on the swelling tide
for those who come.

*   *   *

74

The Rise In The Night

It should be warm tonight
but there is a chill that comes
up from the ground through my legs
and my hands are like dead flowers
with the last color leaving.

All the houses are low and far away
and if there is a light on
I cannot tell it from the gray cat,

and if there were voices at my back
when the sky was like a weeping flower
they have given way to the chattering leaves
and the miles of slow turning worms at my feet.

All week it has rained
and it has rained so much
that I began to feel how full of water
the dead must be,
I began to feel with my eyes
and they told me that when the clouds
break like an ocean
the ground is two lips that part
and everything crawls out.

Tonight this field is drying
and everything is dying back
everything is a nerve that is open

and I can hear them,
the snakes breathing through the green
the chinks and bulbs hissing in their husks
the vines the crawling vines you never see,
they are bleeding from the air
and I hear them.

And there is a low snoring
that is more than the wind,
a low snoring that is my father
in his dark bed
making a gust with his parting nose,
wheezing with his slow veins
beneath a pile of blossoms and bark

and there is a low sound, a prowling snout
that rises up inside my legs and through
my stomach, raising its head into my chest—
and I hear—

because it has stopped raining
and I can hear my own ears breathing
and the trees settling into their deepest wood,
this Beast with its hair is making
a sound that I know,

and it will find its two legs,
and carry a ton of mud
and roots, worms, and the shiny beetles,
and it will carry the legs of my cousins
and my grandmother's shoes—

It will rise with my father's crawling
veins and with iridescent stones,
with the eyes of animals still clear
like water—

and my breathing self will spread
and open like this night.

That Is Why This Day Passes Like A Thousand Lilies

There are whole days of light
that are sad,
there are high trees on the far slope
and small beds of lilies
that give back the day
and make the windows tremble.
There is an outline to the hills
that aches like a woman's body,

and there are gullies on the slopes
I cannot see
small water for the trees
to sink in.

That is why this day passes
like a thousand lilies
and why I stay inside and breathe
too fast.

Outside the pavement smells
of small flowers and petroleum.
The moss shines on spiders and ants.
There is a quiet to the alley that trails
off to the fat woman shouting at her dog,
and for that I stay inside
and listen to the floor boards.

It is not just the light passing
that makes the cows sound far and heavy
and moves me from corner to corner of this room
beckoning me to shout at the onions on the shelf
and laugh at the tomatoes growing old on the sill

but the way the nearest hills
go darker than the trees they lose
and the sleepy flax drones around
the ankles of the farmers,
that leaves my heart shouting at my chest
and my smallest veins weeping
for the trees they never hear

that keeps me with the cupboards full of cans
and dishes, and the long squashes
by the window going soft,
that keeps me here standing over my empty shoes.

Notes

In The Turkish Ward: Siamanto, Armenian poet (1878-1915) was killed by Turkish security agents. His last book of poems, *Bloody News From My Friend,* was based on his correspondence with my grandfather.

The Claim: The documentary portions of this poem have been taken from my grandmother's suit against the Turkish government for losses suffered as a result of the genocide of 1915. The document is titled: *Claims Against Foreign Governments* and was issued by The Department of State, Washington, DC, May 19, 1919 and was executed by her attorney in Newark, New Jersey. She began filing the claim upon her arrival in Aleppo, Syria, after the deportation, during which time she was living under the protection of the U.S. Consulate.

Diarbekir is an ancient Armenian city, with a fortress of walls around it, located in southeastern Turkey.

About the author

Peter Balakian was born in 1951 in Teaneck, New Jersey and grew up there and in the neighboring town of Tenafly. He holds a B.A. from Bucknell University and a Ph.D. from Brown. He is co-editor of *Graham House Review* which he founded with Bruce Smith in 1976. He is a member of the English department at Colgate; his first book, *Father Fisheye*, was published in 1979.